AUSTRIAN
NARROW GAUGE

John Organ

Series editor Vic Mitchell

MP Middleton Press

Front Cover: Krauss, Linz 0-10-0T no. Kh 101, dating from 1926, was working hard at Bachl on the Feistritztalbahn with a tourist train from Weiz to Birkfeld, when it was photographed on 5th August 1993. (Miss S. Benn)

Rear Cover: SLM 0-4-2RT rack and pinion locomotive no. 999.202 was built in 1992. It is seen at St. Wolfgang on the Schafbergbahn on 21st May 2001. The Abt rack gear from one of the earlier Krauss locomotives decorates the buffer stops. (J.A.Foster)

First Published September 2003

ISBN 1 904474 04 7

© *Middleton Press, 2003*

Design   David Pede
Typesetting   Barbara Mitchell

Published by
          Middleton Press
          Easebourne Lane
          Midhurst, West Sussex
          GU29 9AZ
Tel: 01730 813169
Fax: 01730 812601
Email: info@middletonpress.co.uk
www.middletonpress.co.uk

Printed & bound by Biddles Ltd, Kings Lynn

CONTENTS

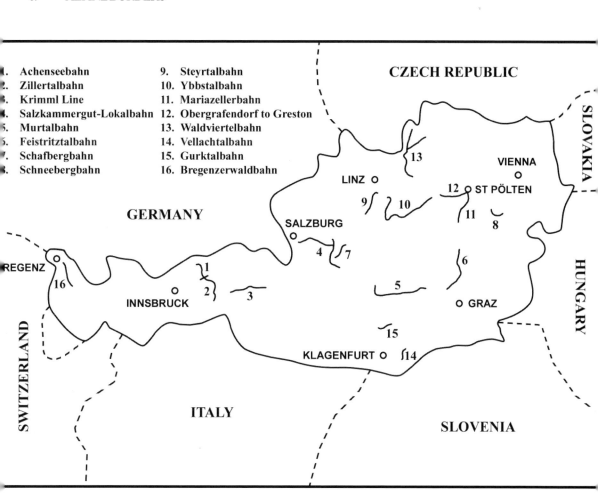

INTRODUCTION

The mountain chain known collectively as The Alps runs from South East France, across the entire length of Southern Switzerland and finally much of Southern Austria. Also embraced is the northern area of Italy and part of Slovenia, much of which was formerly under Austrian control prior to the boundary changes following World War 1.

Like Switzerland, Austria was interlaced with an amazing network of Narrow Gauge Railways. However the situation here is slightly different. Apart from three metre gauge rack and pinion lines, two of which are operated by the Austrian State Railways / *Österreichisch Bundesbahnen (ÖBB)*, 76cm was chosen for the majority of narrow gauge routes. Many were part of the state network whilst there were also some extensive privately owned systems. Some of the latter currently remain in operation with modern railcars and diesel locomotives. In addition, a number of metre gauge electric routes were opened throughout the country. These largely fall into the category of urban tramway systems and consequently are outside the scope of this publication.

Austria never adopted electrification of its minor railways to such a large extent as Switzerland. Consequently steam hauled trains remained a regular feature of everyday services until quite recently. Due to rationalisation of local transport, many of the ÖBB narrow gauge lines have closed during the last two decades. Those that have survived have been modernised using diesel traction for both passenger and freight operations. However steam has remained as an attraction for tourist trains on a number of the privately owned lines, with varying degrees of utilisation. Additionally there exist some very committed preservation groups, which operate their locomotives both on dedicated museum lines and also in conjunction with the commercial operations for their tourist trains.

As in Switzerland, the majority of Austrian narrow gauge locomotives were the products of one manufacturer. *Lokomotiv-Fabrik Krauss*, Linz, will feature regularly in this publication, along with its associated Munich based concern. After the Linz works were closed in 1930, all subsequent Austrian narrow gauge locomotives were constructed by *Wiener Lokomotiv-Fabrik AG,* Floridsdorf, Vienna (Wien).

This book will attempt to cover the major narrow gauge steam operations in the alpine regions of Austria. Using archive views and current scenes on some of these scenic lines, the flavour of the contrasting systems of this fascinating country will be most apparent. The narrow gauge lines of Switzerland are featured in a companion volume, *Swiss Narrow Gauge*.

ACKNOWLEDGEMENTS

As usual in a book of this kind, it could not have been completed without the invaluable help of many people. My thanks are due to Mr and Mrs B. Benn, Miss. S. Benn, Mr. J. A. Foster, Monsieur B. Gueret (BVA), Mr. P. Hay, Mr. A. Heywood, Mr. N. Langridge, Mr. J. Marsh, Mr. J. Mills, Mr. D. Trevor Rowe, Mr. D. Smith, Mr. K. Taylorson and Mr. J.K.Williams. Finally I must add a special word of thanks to my wife Brenda, who has once again tolerated my deep involvement in the subject during the period of research and compilation.

1. AUSTRIAN NARROW GAUGE STEAM LOCOMOTIVES

As an introduction to this survey of the steam operations on the many narrow gauge railways of Austria, a brief history of the development of motive power on these systems follows.

The majority of narrow gauge locomotives were built between 1888 and 1930 by *Lokomotiv-Fabrik Krauss,* Linz, whilst others were the products of *Wiener Lokomotiv-Fabrik AG,* Floridsdorf, Vienna. The latter were more commonly associated with standard gauge motive power, but took over the production of narrow gauge locomotives following the closure of the Linz works in 1930. During the early years of the 20th Century, some of the Linz production was subcontracted to the *Actien-Gesellschaft der Lokomotiv-Fabrik* works at Wiener Neustadt. Following the *Lokalbahn Legislation* of 1887, which resulted in the construction of numerous 76cm railways, a basically standard type of locomotive was designed by the Linz works, although there were a number of variations on the theme.

The first 0-6-2Ts were the "*Steyrtalbahn Loks*", built between 1888 and 1894 for use on the *Steyrtalbahn* and similar locomotives for the *Salzkammergut-Lokalbahn.* Known unofficially as the "S Class", the earliest examples had extra long smoke boxes extending well beyond the chimney line, resulting in a most unusual appearance. Later versions had more conventional smoke boxes and a larger boiler capacity. These locomotives were fitted with 800mm driving wheels, 290 x 400mm cylinders, 40.15 sq. metres of heating surface and 0.80 sq. metres of grate area. Between 1898 and 1902 a smaller version, the T Class, was introduced for use in Carinthia. These had 640mm driving wheels and 260 x 300mm cylinders. Prior to the introduction of the T Class, three 0-6-0Ts of similar dimensions had been supplied to the *Steiermärkische Landesbahnen* in 1892 and four more were supplied to the *Pinzgauerbahn* in 1898. Known as the Z Class, these were the only examples of that wheel arrangement built at Linz.

The most numerous type of 76cm 0-6-2T locomotive to be produced at Linz was the U Class. These were delivered between 1894 and 1922 and 61 were supplied to the majority of railways throughout the country. Some were "lost" to Italy and Yugoslavia following the boundary changes after WW 1. The wheels and cylinder dimensions were the same as the "S Class" but the boilers were larger. These had 46.3 sq. metres of heating surface and 1 sq. metre of grate area. The U Class was distinguishable from the earlier locomotives by their full-length tanks, the front of which were in line with the smokebox door. Between 1902 and 1905, a compound version known as the Uv Class was introduced. These had cylinders of 320 and 500 x 400mm, plus a larger boiler with 57.8 square metres of heating surface.

All members of both the "S" and U Class, including the Uv variants, which were absorbed into the ÖBB network, were known as the 298 Class. This would no doubt have also applied to the T Class, although these were all withdrawn at an early date. Some of the later members of both variants of the U Class, produced after 1902, were fitted with a rear coal - bunker, in addition to the original small bunker in front of the cab on the fireman's side. The final "S Class" locomotive, supplied in 1906, was also fitted with this modification. During their active careers, many of the U Class locomotives have sported a large spark-arresting device on their chimneys. These additions, that look like a large flower pot, are typically Austrian in their appearance. As they appear only to have been fitted to the U Class, presumably they were particularly prone to throwing sparks!

Prior to the introduction of the Uv Class, three Compound 0-6-4Ts had been delivered in 1896. Known as the Yv Class, they spent all their working lives on the *Ybbstalbahn*, where two remain in the care of "Club 598". One is in working order and the other currently under overhaul. The third member is preserved as a static exhibit at Eichgraben in Carinthia. These were derived from the *Steyrtalbahn Loks*, and in some ways were prototypes for the Uv Class. Their dimensions were similar to the latter whilst the ÖBB classification was the 598 Class.

In 1905, Krauss Linz produced a superheated version of the U Class with piston valves. This sole example was originally known as a type Uh, later to be referred to as type Bh to distinguish it from later machines. It is currently preserved as Bh1, but ran in ÖBB service as 398.01.

Rather surprisingly, despite the success of this prototype machine, a production version did not appear until 1928. This was the Uh Class, which turned out to be the final and arguably finest design to emerge from Linz. These were much larger than the previous 0-6-2Ts weighing 28.1 tonnes with 44 sq. metres of heating surface and 1.06 sq. metres of grate area. These last products from Linz were fitted with Caprotti valve gear whilst the two final examples, built at Floridsdorf in 1931, had Lentz Poppet Valve Gear. The distinction of being the last locomotive built at Linz, is held by no.5 of the *Zillertalbahn* (works no.1521) which was delivered in 1930. The Caprotti valve gear on no.5 was replaced in 1941 by the Lentz arrangement. In ÖBB service, the Uh type was known as the 498 Class.

In addition to the various 0-6-2T types, some successful 0-8+4 superheated Engerth locomotives were introduced in 1906. The Mh Class was originally supplied to the steeply graded *Mariazellerbahn* and were transferred to the *Waldviertalbahn*, following the electrification of the St.Polten to Mariazell line in 1911. The Engerth design, which is really a 0-8-0 with a permanently close coupled tender with sliding arm attachments on each side of the firebox, have proved to be an excellent machine in service. The advantage of the Engerth design is that running tender first, normally avoided wherever possible on European lines, is permitted without any problems of stability. Known as the 399 Class, they were fitted with 900mm driving wheels, 410 x 450mm cylinders, 78.8 sq. metres of heating surface and 1.60 sq. metres of grate area. Six locomotives of this type were built between 1906 and 1908, all of which are still in existence.

Between the two batches of Mh locomotives, two compound versions of the Engerths were supplied in 1907.Known as the Mv Class, or ÖBB 299, they had 370 and 500mm diameter cylinders and 95.04 sq. metres of heating surface. Unlike the superheated locomotives, the compound variants did not survive, being withdrawn in 1962 and 1965. They were initially based at St. Pölten, for use on the line to Gresten, before being transferred to the *Waldviertalbahn* for the majority of their remaining careers. They both returned to Obergrafenendorf in 1961 shortly before their withdrawal. No. 299.02 survived in derelict condition at Knittelfeld Works until 1995, when it was used as the basis for a snowplough for use on the *Ybbstalbahn*. 299.01 had suffered a similar fate some years earlier.

Another successful superheated design to emerge from Linz was the 0-10-0T Kh Class, three of which were built between 1924 and 1930. In order to traverse tight radius curves, these locomotives had four axles with inside frames whilst the rear axle was within splayed outside frames with liberal provision for lateral movement provided by the *Klien Lindner* system. The first member of the class became ÖBB no. 499.01, for service in Carinthia, whilst the others were supplied to the *Steiermärkische Landesbahnen* as nos. Kh 101 and Kh 111. The last one was fitted with Caprotti valve gear, and all three have been preserved.

Similar in appearance to the Kh type was the P Class 0-8-2T. Three were originally built in 1911 for the *Trieste-Parenzo* line, which was ceded to Italy after 1918. Three more were built for the BBÖ (predecessor of the ÖBB) Obergrafendorf to Gresten line in 1926. These were later to be known as the 199 Class.

All subsequent locomotives acquired for use on the Austrian 76cm lines were imported from elsewhere, mainly Germany or France. A large number were supplied to the German armed forces during WW 2 for their *Heeresfeldbahn* systems, and were requisitioned following the end of the war. In view of the fact that the German lines were 75cm gauge, some slight re-gauging was necessary to these locomotives before entering service. A number of these were fitted during the 1950s with Austria's most famous contribution to locomotive development, the Giesl Ejector chimney. The majority of these newly acquired locomotives were Franco-Belge KDL 11 type 0-8-0s of either Tender/Tank or Tank variations. Those of both types, which entered service on the state system, received the ÖBB designation of 699 Class. The other acquisitions were mainly 0-6-0TTs built by a variety of German manufacturers and a solitary Borsig 0-10-0TT. None of these went to the state lines and consequently did not receive a ÖBB class number.

The metre gauge rack and pinion lines used examples of three manufacturers. These included four 0-4-0RTs built at Floridsdorf in 1889, ten 0-4-2RTs from Linz between 1893 and 1900, and four of the SLM oil fired 0-4-2RTs supplied in 1992, similar to those at work in Switzerland. The Linz built rack engines, used on the ÖBB lines, were also fitted with Giesl Ejectors during the second half of their long careers. These became the 999.0 and 999.1 classes, whilst the later Swiss built machines were designated as the 999.2 type.

1.1   This is no.4, one of the first 0-6-2Ts supplied to the Salzkammergut-Lokalbahn in 1894. This view shows the extended smokebox, which was fitted to the earlier SKGLB and Steyrtalbahn locomotives, when it was photographed at Salzburg in 1953. (Ing.K.Kreibich – J.F. Organ coll.)

1.2   One of the ubiquitous U Class 0-6-2Ts, that were used on almost every 76cm gauge line in Austria. Zillertalbahn no.2, built at Linz in 1900, was photographed at Jenbach in May 1985 fitted with a spark-arresting chimney. (J. Marsh)

1.3 *Compound Uv Class 0-6-2T, Zillertalbahn no.3, stands at Jenbach in September 1990. This view of the powerful locomotive, built in 1902, shows the high-pressure side with the smaller cylinder. (J.F. Organ)*

1.4 *This was the last locomotive to be supplied by Krauss, Linz in 1930. Superheated Uh Class 0-6-2T no.5 of the ZB was photographed at Jenbach in May 1985. This locomotive was originally fitted with Caprotti valve gear, which was replaced by the Lentz Poppet gear fitted in 1941. (J. Marsh)*

1.5 *0-10-0T no. Kh 111 of 1930 vintage is seen at Mauterndorf in September 1958, which at the time was the western terminus of the* **Murtalbahn** *(StLB). Note the rear pair of driving wheels within the splayed outside frames and the Caprotti valve gear. (D.Trevor Rowe)*

1.6   Engerth Mh Class 0-8+4 no. 399.01 stands outside the depot at Zell am See in September 1990. The close-coupled tender of this design, introduced by Krauss, Linz in 1906, is clearly shown in this view. The locomotive was being prepared for an excursion to Krimml the following day. (J.F.Organ)

2. THREE GAUGES AT JENBACH.

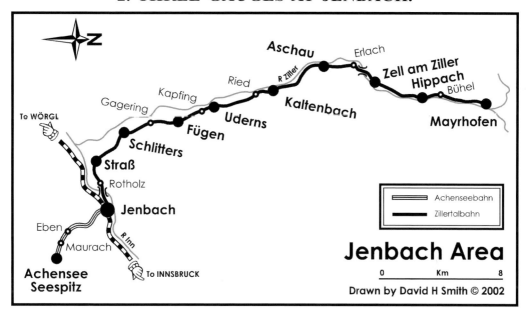

The first chapter of the Swiss volume in this series began at Montreux, where lines of three gauges converge in one station. Appropriately, the Austrian survey commences at Jenbach, a small town in the Tirol about 30 km east of Innsbruck, where three gauges also meet. Jenbach is also the home of the *Jenbacher Werke*, the long established builder of industrial diesel and electric locomotives. Through the extensive main line station run the metals of the standard gauge ÖBB route linking Innsbruck with Salzburg and Vienna, which connects with the Arlberg and Brenner routes at Innsbruck and the main line to Munich, which diverts from the Salzburg line at Wörgl.

Each side of this busy station two contrasting narrow gauge lines, that have served the area since the turn of the 20th Century, have their operational headquarters. Although both now heavily rely upon tourist traffic for the majority of their business, they were originally constructed to provide a service for the communities along their respective routes.

Achenseebahn

The first of the two lines at Jenbach is the metre gauge Riggenbach rack and pinion route, which climbs for 7km to a lakeside upper terminus at the 931m. Achensee. However the actual summit is about half way along its route at Eben, 970m.above sea level. Opened in 1889, three of the original 0-4-0RT locomotives, built at Floridsdorf, are still in use. A fourth member of the class was cannibalised for spare parts some years ago.

Unlike most rack and pinion lines, which terminate at an upper summit station, the *Achenseebahn* is a combination of rack and adhesion sections despite the use of locomotives with a steeply inclined boiler. Leaving the station yard at Jenbach, the rack is engaged immediately for the climb to Eben. Initially the gradient is at 1 in 10 but soon increases to 1 in 5 as the vintage locomotive works noisily, amid clouds of black smoke, as it pushes its two four wheeled coaches up the incline surrounded by woodland.

Approaching the station at Eben, the regulator is closed and the two coaches, that are not coupled to the locomotive, glide gracefully to a halt at the platform. The points are then changed and the locomotive runs through the loop and couples onto the front carriage in the conventional manner.

The remainder of the journey via Maurach to the Achensee Seespitz terminus, where passengers can transfer to a lake steamer, is completed on a conventional track, the locomotive presenting a bizarre sight with its steeply angled boiler and cab perched high above the carriages. The valve motion is linked to an external idler wheel, which is connected to the rack mechanism. This idler wheel and the valve gear revolves in the opposite direction to the driving wheels and coupling rods, thereby adding to the strange sight of one of these venerable machines in action.

This interesting railway operates an intensive service between May and September. As well as being situated at the summit of the rack section, Eben is also the passing place for up and down trains. At busy periods of operation, this station can witness some intense activity. Alternatively, all three trains often converge at the lakeside terminus simultaneously, where some intricate shunting is required in view of the limited platform facilities.

Die Zillertalbahn

On the southern side of Jenbach station is the extensive station, depot and workshops complex of one of the best known Austrian 76cm lines. Opened between 1900 and 1902, this 32km line is operated by an enterprising organisation known as *Zillertaler Verkehrsbetrieb AG,* which in addition to the railway also runs a bus service and a travel agency. Running through the Ziller Valley to the winter sports centre of Mayrhofen, a year round service is provided, not only for the many tourists that converge on this area for both summer and winter pursuits, but also as a local means of transport. In addition an extensive freight service is provided, with standard gauge wagons carried on 76cm transporter vehicles. The main freight carried is timber from the extensive yard at Fügen-Hart and products of an engineering works near Mayrhofen. The railway played an important role in transporting building materials and heavy machinery for a power station that was constructed near Mayrhofen during the 1960s. This operation entailed building an access line to the works site.

The route of the *Zillertalbahn* (ZB) follows the valley floor during its journey from Jenbach, and is consequently devoid of many major civil engineering features. The two largest structures are the girder bridges at Rotholz and Zell am Ziller where the River Inn and River Ziller are crossed respectively. The major intermediate stations are at Schlitters, Fügen, Kaltenbach and Zell am Ziller, plus a number of line-side halts along the route.

Two U Class locomotives built at Linz were supplied for the opening of the first section of the line between Jenbach and Fügen in 1900. Of these, no.2 is still in service whilst no.1 has for some years resided in a transport museum at Innsbruck. It was returned to Jenbach in 2002, as part of the centenary celebrations of the ZB, and it is possible that it will be restored to working order in due course. Following the completion of the line to Mayrhofen in 1902, the two 0-6-2Ts were joined by a compound Uv Class locomotive. No.3 is still in active service on the line, sharing the haulage of lighter trains with no.2. In 1905, the three 0-6-2Ts were joined by a small 2-4-0T, which was primarily engaged for shunting at Jenbach, or piloting one of its larger sisters on heavy trains. This unusual locomotive from Linz, was in appearance a shorter version of a U Class, but of course with a completely different wheel and cylinder arrangement. Unfortunately, this unique machine was withdrawn from service in 1958 and presumably scrapped.

In 1930, the last locomotive to be constructed at the Krauss Linz works was supplied to the ZB.

This was no.5, a superheated Uh Class 0-6-2T, which was an invaluable investment due to the increased tonnage being carried by that time. Originally fitted with Caprotti valve gear, it was rebuilt in 1941 with Lentz poppet valve gear.

Following the closure of the *Salzkammergut-Lokalbahn* (SKGLB) in 1957, a number of surplus locomotives became available. With increasing freight traffic, the ZB acquired a 0-10-0TT, tender/tank machine, built by Borsig in 1939. This large and powerful locomotive had been used during WW 2 by the German armed forces and requisitioned by the SKGLB in 1945. Used mainly for freight trains, the

2.1　　Achenseebahn *0-4-0RT no.3 prepares to depart from Jenbach. The idler gear connecting the valve gear to the rack mechanism, which revolves in the reverse direction to the wheels and motion, is clearly seen in this photograph captured in May 1985. (J. Marsh)*

2.2　　*The frames of one of the 0-4-0RTs were seen in the workshop at Jenbach on the same occasion. Four, identical, locomotives were supplied by Floridsdorf for the opening of the line in 1889, three of which remain in service. The moped was presumably not in for a refit at the same time! (J. Marsh)*

2.3 The initial gradient after leaving Jenbach is 1 in 10, where one of the 0-4-0RTs was viewed ascending the climb, before it increases to 1 in 5 for the remainder of the route to Eben. (D. Trevor Rowe)

2.4 No. 3 was photographed approaching the summit of the incline at Eben on 4th September 1990. The sound of the locomotive climbing through the trees in the background, long before it came into view, was very dramatic. (J.F. Organ).

2.5.   The summit station at Eben is seen on the same occasion, as no.3 propels its two coaches into the passing loop, before the locomotive runs round the train prior to continuing its journey to Seespitz. (J.F. Organ).

2.6   No.2 and a single coach train waits at Eben, before the locomotive runs through the loop, in May 1985. Unique among alpine rack and pinion mountain lines, the Achenseebahn incorporates a section of adhesion line between the summit and terminus. (J. Marsh).

2.7   With the driver perched in an elevated position, no.2 is seen traversing the loop at Eben before hauling its train to the lakeside terminus in May 1985. (J. Marsh).

2.8   When viewed on the level, separated from the rolling stock, the Floridsdorf built 0-4-0RTs appear somewhat ungainly with their inclined boilers and cabs. Even more surprising is the fact that the adhesion section from Eben is on a slight descent, with the result that the inclined boilers are at an even greater angle. (J. Marsh).

2.9   *A busy scene was recorded at Eben, as two trains pass on 27th June 1970. No.2 has just arrived from Jenbach whilst no.3 is returning from the upper terminus, before the final descent on the rack section. (J.K.Williams).*

2.10   *0-4-0RT no.1 hauls a single coach RCTS special along the upper adhesion section of the* **Achenseebahn** *in June 1970. This view again accentuates the angle of the inclined boiler and cabs of these historic locomotives. (J.K.Williams).*

2.11   *Nearing the terminus, no.2 coasts down the grade near Maurach. The Riggenbach gear pinion is clearly visible below the locomotive in this view photographed on 29th August 1984. (D. Trevor Rowe)*

2.12   *No.2 arrives at the lakeside terminus at Seespitz on 4th September 1990. Due to the limited space at this location, much complex shunting is necessary when more than one train is in the station. (J.F. Organ)*

2.13   *0-4-0RT no.2 was seen at Maurach with a train returning to Jenbach on 29ᵗʰ August 1984. The upper section of the* Achenseebahn *is more akin to a rural branch line than a mountain railway.   (D. Trevor Rowe)*

2.14   *A very heavily loaded train prepares to depart from Jenbach to Mayrhofen, double headed by 0-6-2Ts nos 3 and 5. Trains of this length are quite common during the peak season on the* Zillertalbahn, *such as this one photographed on 13ᵗʰ August 1992. (B. Benn)*

*2.15   Contrasting locomotives from Linz. Uh Class 0-6-2T no.5 is seen in the foreground, whilst U Class no.2 stands alongside the coal stage, when viewed at Jenbach depot in May 1985.
(J. Marsh)*

*2.16   No.5 was seen reversing through the yard, prior to coupling onto the rolling stock in the background. The linkage for the Lentz valve gear is clearly seen on the side of the cylinder casing.
(J. Marsh)*

2.17   The valve motion of U Class 0-6-2T no.2 receives a final oiling, before hauling a train to *Mayrhofen in May 1985. This is one of the two original locomotives supplied to the ZB in 1900. (J. Marsh)*

2.18   **The Zillertalbahn's** *pioneer 0-6-2T, no.1, was photographed at Jenbach on 16th January 1961. This locomotive, built at Linz in 1900, was confined to a transport museum at Innsbruck in the 1980s. It was returned to Jenbach in 2002 as part of the centenary celebrations of the* **Zillertalbahn.** *(P. Hay)*

2.19   This unique Krauss, Linz 2-4-0T no.4, was used for shunting and light duties by the ZB until 1958. This diminutive locomotive, built in 1905, was seen at Jenbach in 1956. (P. Hay)

2.20   Another view of 2-4-0T no.4; it was photographed on shunting duty at Jenbach during the 1950s. Following its withdrawal, the number was transferred to the Borsig 0-10-0 TT acquired from the SKGLB in 1958. (J.K.Williams)

2.21   On a cold winter day in January 1961, U Class no.1, hauling a train bound for Mayrhofen, passes Uh Class no.5 returning to Jenbach, at Schlitters.   The Zillertalbahn locomotives have always worked facing Mayrhofen, there being no turntables on the line. (P. Hay)

2.22   In complete contrast, on a hot summer afternoon, Uv Class 0-6-2T no.3 hauls a train bound for Mayrhofen through the meadows near Kaltenbach on 12th August 1992. (Miss. S. Benn)

2.23   Uv Class no.3 is seen approaching the bridge spanning the Ziller River near Zell am Ziller, hauling a heavily laden morning train from Jenbach on 5th September 1990. (J.F. Organ)

2.24   Another aspect of the Zillertalbahn motive power. Former Yugoslavian BoBo Diesel Hydraulic, no.10, stands alongside one of the Knotz/BBC railcar sets at Zell am Ziller. The railcars handle most of the regular passenger traffic, the large diesel locomotives being normally employed for freight services. However, they are sometimes seen hauling passenger trains, as on this occasion on 5th September 1990. (J.F. Organ)

*2.25   U Class 0-6-2T no.1 is seen approaching the winter sports resort of Mayrhofen amid fresh snow in January 1961. At this time, the **Zillertalbahn** passenger services were entirely steam hauled. (P. Hay)*

2.26   No.3 waits in the compact station at Mayrhofen, before hauling the return morning train to Jenbach on 4th September 1990. The daily steam hauled trains are a very popular attraction on this delightful railway in the Tirol, in both summer and winter. (J.F. Organ)

2.27   Another winter scene as 0-6-2T no.3 was photographed arriving at Mayrhofen on 3rd January 1994. The two contrasting diameters of the compound cylinders of the Uv Class are clearly seen in this view. (B. Benn)

2.28   U Class no.2 was viewed replenishing its water tanks at the upper terminus in May 1985. The simple and efficient "water tower" is a characteristic feature of the Austrian narrow gauge lines. (J. Marsh)

2.29   *Another view of Uh Class no.5 shows it arriving at Mayrhofen in January 1961. At this period steam was still in daily use on all trains, the diesels had yet to arrive. (P. Hay)*

2.30   *Uv Class no.3 and the Borsig 0-10-0TT no.4 prepare to depart from Mayrhofen on the same occasion. Even during the early 1960s, double heading was necessary on many trains due to the heavy patronage of the services. (P. Hay)*

2.31   U Class no.1 waits at Mayrhofen, whilst the mail is transferred to the waiting post van in January 1961. In addition to the tourist traffic, the ZB has always provided a service to the local community. (P. Hay)

2.32   This powerful 83 Class 0-8-2 tender locomotive no. 83.076, although built at Linz in 1909, spent the majority of its working life in the former Yugoslavia. Now returned to Austria in the care of "Club 760", it has been on long term loan to the Zillertalbahn during the last decade. It was photographed preparing to depart from Jenbach with a heavy train on 20th July 2002. (K. Taylorson)

2.33   ÖBB 0-6-2T no.298.05 arrives at Zell am See, with an early morning train from Krimml on 8th September 1956. This would have provided a commuter service for the many villages along the Pinzgau Valley, which is still provided today but using diesel railcars rather than steam haulage. (P. Hay)

2.34   U Class no.298.51 prepares to depart from Zell am See with a mixed train on 14th September 1956. A standard gauge wagon on a transporter vehicle is visible in the distance, whilst a narrow gauge diesel locomotive is seen to the right of the photograph. Note the interlaced tracks on which the train is positioned. (P. Hay)

2.35　*The same train was photographed, shortly after leaving Zell am See, running through a typical alpine valley. The standard gauge wagon at the rear of the train is clearly seen in this view. (P. Hay)*

2.36　*Mh Class 0-8+4 no. 399.01 hauls a steam special towards Krimml along the valley near Neukirchen on 11th August 1992. A modern ÖBB coach is included in the formation along with a variety of rolling stock of an earlier vintage. (Miss. S. Benn)*

2.37   The current daily services are worked by diesel powered machines as illustrated in this photograph. Since their introduction in 1986, the railcars have allowed the introduction of a far more intensive timetable. A 2095 Class B-B locomotive and a 5090 Class railcar stand at Krimml on 7th September 1990, prior to returning their respective trains to Zell am See. (J.F. Organ)

3. DIE SALZKAMMERGUT-LOKALBAHN

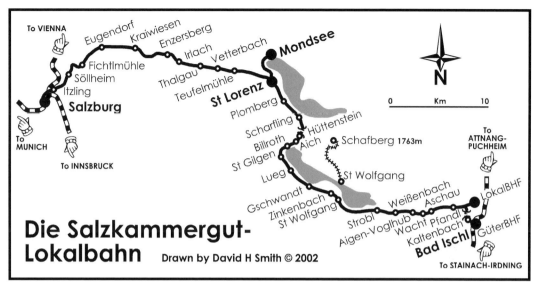

Of the many independent narrow gauge lines in Austria, the 67 km *Salzkammergut-Lokalbahn* (SKGLB) in the "Lake District" south of Salzburg, was the most scenic. Sadly, it was also the first to close. Opened in stages between 1890 and 1894 to serve the many villages along the route between Salzburg and Bad Ischl, it connected with two major main line railways at each terminal. Following the upheaval of World War 2 and the increase in the use of road transport, the SKGLB succumbed to rationalisation of local transport and closed on 30th September 1957. Had it survived into the next decade, it would surely have been saved, in part if not wholly, and became an established part of the European railway preservation movement.

The first section of the route to open in 1890 was the 9km from Bad Ischl to Strobl on the shore of the *Wolfgangsee*, one of the largest lakes in the area. The following year a 31.6km line from Salzburg to Mondsee, on the shore of a lake of the same name, opened. With two isolated sections of railway, it was obvious that they should be connected at the earliest opportunity. The difficult terrain between the two lakes was finally overcome by June 1893 when the 22.5km section, including a summit tunnel, opened between Strobl and St.Lorenz where a junction was created with the Mondsee line. Thus the 5km between St.Lorenz and Mondsee became a branch line. The final link in the chain was added 12 months later. Following the construction of a tunnel through the high ground to the west of Bad Ischl, a 3.8km line connecting the original terminus at Bad Ischl with the main line station was opened in July 1894. The final 1km of this connection was interlaced with the tracks of the standard gauge route that links Attnang-Puchheim in the north with Stainach-Irdning to the south.

The journey from Salzburg to Bad Ischl was one of contrasts. Leaving the terminus at Salzburg, situated at a lower level than the busy main line station, it passed under the standard gauge line to Vienna before negotiating numerous sidings and yards of both gauges. There then followed a journey through a pleasant rural area of agricultural land until the gateway to the Alpine region was reached at St.Lorenz. Here the short branch along the shore of the *Mondsee* left the "main line" to reach its terminus at the northern end of the lake.

Departing from St.Lorenz the SKGLB ran along the southern shore of the *Mondsee* to Scharfling before a steep climb through woodland to the summit of the line at Hüttenstein was ascended. The summit was traversed via a short tunnel, in a delightful setting among the trees, before the descent to the shore of the *Wolfgangsee* at St.Gilgen. The remainder of the route to Strobl followed the southern shore of this beautiful lake surrounded by mountains. The station at St.Wolfgang was on the opposite shore to that of the village it served, so a short trip by ferry across a narrow neck of the lake was necessary. The village at St.Wolfgang is the location of the famous "White Horse Inn" and the lower terminus of the metre gauge rack and pinion line to the Schafberg. This line was originally operated by the SKGLB until it was transferred to the state in 1939 during the German occupation of Austria. The Schafberg line will be covered in a later chapter.

From Strobl, the oldest part of the SKGLB was traversed along the floor of the valley via the villages of Aschau and Pfandl. Shortly before the original station at Bad Ischl was reached, the line turned sharply right and burrowed through the mountain behind the town via a 670m.tunnel. At the south of Bad Ischl, the 76cm line joined the standard gauge metals and entered the main line station after crossing a bow shaped steel girder-bridge.

Locomotives of the SKGLB

Unlike the majority of its contemporaries, the SKGLB possessed a very varied assortment of motive power. For the opening of the line in 1890, Krauss Linz supplied two 0-4-0Ts for the initial short and easily graded route between Bad Ischl and Strobl. Nos 1 and 2 were mainly used for shunting and other light duties following the connection with the remainder of the system. In 1918, no.1 was despatched to Romania whilst no.2 remained at Salzburg until 1953. One of their regular duties was on the short Mondsee branch, which was shared with a railcar.

Following the opening of the remaining sections of the SKGLB, between 1891 and 1894, a total of nine 0-6-2Ts, similar to the first *Steyertalbahn Loks*, were supplied from Linz. These locomotives, nos 3 to 11, were to become synonymous with the line, with another (no.12) being supplied in 1906. Nos 3, 4 and 5 were of the earlier design with the long smoke-box projecting in front of the chimney. During World War 1, nos 3, 4, 5 and 8 were requisitioned for war service. No.4 went to Italy whilst the others were despatched to Bosnia. Nos 3 and 4 returned home in 1921, but the others were destined never to return to the railway, although no.5 has been repatriated in recent years by "Club 760".

To bolster the depleted stock, two further locomotives were acquired in 1925 and 1928. The first was a unique compound 0-8-0T built by Krauss in 1923 whilst the other was a superheated 0-10-0T Well-Tank built by Maffei, at Munich in 1920 for a forestry line near Konstanz. These two powerful additions were mainly used on freight trains, although they were also assigned to passenger duties on occasions. In 1942 a pair of Orenstein and Koppel 0-6-0Ts, dating from 1940, were added to the locomotive stock.

Following World War 2, many surplus locomotives from the occupying forces military railways depot at Mittersill became available. Consequently four additional machines were acquired which proved to be a great asset during the final decade of the SKGLB's existence. These included a Franco-Belge KDL 11 type 0-8-0TT, a Borsig 0-10-0TT and a pair of 0-6-0TTs built by Böhmisch (B.M.F) and Henschel. From the same source, a Deutz diesel locomotive was also acquired for shunting duties.

The Deutz wasn't the first internal combustion vehicle on the SKGLB. In 1928 a petrol-electric railcar was built by Gebus, adapted from a saloon coach no.S 51, which spent most of its life on the short branch between St.Lorenz and Mondsee. In 1933, three much more powerful diesel railcars built by Austro Daimler were supplied. However, their life on the SKGLB was short, being transferred to the *Steiermärkische Landesbahnen* in 1939. The StLB were to acquire much of the SKGLB locomotive fleet in 1957, resulting in the continued survival of these locomotives.

Three of the 0-6-2Ts, nos 7, 11 and 12 went to the StLB along with the Franco-Belge KDL 11 type 0-8-0TT no.19, which was subsequently re-sold to the Welshpool and Llanfair. The Deutz diesel shunter and the Gebus railcar were also transferred to the StLB following the closure. The Borsig 0-10-0TT, no.22, went initially to the *Zillertalbahn* but, as recorded in the previous chapter, has now returned to the country of its manufacture.

The passenger rolling stock comprised mainly of the usual end balcony four wheeled coaches, as used on all the 76cm lines. However one interesting vehicle was coach 152, which was once the private saloon of Emperor Franz Josef who owned a country retreat near Bad Ischl.

Of the remaining locomotives, 0-6-2Ts nos 4 and 9 were preserved on plinths at Pfandl and Mondsee respectively. These are now housed at the SKGLB museum that is located in the former engine shed at Mondsee. The collection also includes two 0-6-2Ts from the "Club 760" collection, no.5 and no.12, the latter having been repatriated from Germany. Also preserved in the museum is the Franz Josef saloon, now restored to its original condition.

The scene today

Sadly, little remains today of the SKGLB, 45 years after its untimely closure. Due to road improvement schemes, much of the former track bed has disappeared under tarmac whilst urban development in the Salzburg area has obliterated the former route. At Bad Ischl, the station and bridge remain much as it did during the 1950s, but minus the 76cm rails interlaced with the standard gauge track. It is still possible to trace part of the steeply graded route between the two lakes, which has been adapted as a footpath. Even though most of the infrastructure has vanished in the cause of progress, fortunately many of the locomotives and some items of rolling stock survive at various locations in Austria, Germany and Great Britain.

3.1   This is one of the Krauss 0-6-2Ts, that were synonymous with the Salzkammergut-Lokalbahn. No.11, dating from 1894, was photographed at Salzburg depot during the final years of the SKGLB. (J.K.Williams coll.)

3.2.   No.3, one of the first "S Class" locomotives built in 1891, was captured at Salzburg during the 1950s. This example was fitted with a later type boiler and chimney during the 1940s, thereby losing its original extended smoke box. (J.K.Williams coll.)

3.3   This is no.21, the superheated 0-10-0WT, which was built by Maffei at Munich in 1920. Originally supplied to a forestry line near Konstanz, this powerful locomotive was acquired by the SKGLB in 1928 and mainly employed on freight trains. (J.K.Williams coll.)

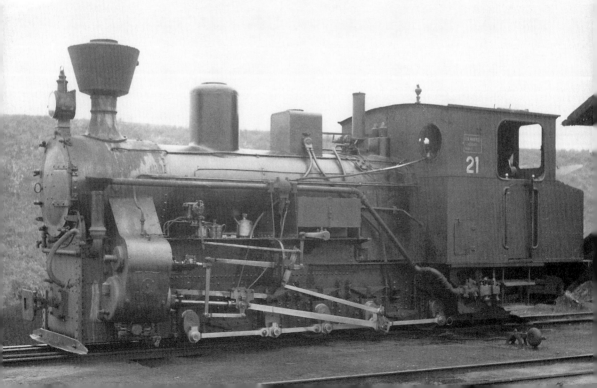

3.4 *0-6-2T no.11 takes on water and fuel at St.Lorenz in September 1956. Despite a lack of investment during the final years of the SKGLB, the equipment and infrastructure appears to be in excellent condition. (P. Hay)*

3.5 *Borsig 0-10-0TT no.22 passes a level crossing at Hüttenstein, whilst hauling a train from Salzburg to Bad Ischl, on 16th September 1956. This locomotive was transferred to the Zillertalbahn in 1958 and became their second no.4. (P. Hay)*

3.6   0-6-2T no.10 was seen leaving the summit tunnel near Hüttenstein, with an early morning train from Salzburg in September 1956. This view emphasises the varied scenery through which this delightful railway passed. (P. Hay)

3.7   "Is there really track there?" The rails have begun to disappear below the undergrowth, whilst No.12 waits at Aich as no. 11 approaches with a train from Salzburg on 15th September 1956. (P. Hay)

3.8 *A few minutes later, no.11 stops at Aich before proceeding to Bad Ischl. It would appear to be collecting some young passengers from the village school. (P. Hay)*

3.9 *0-6-2T no.3 presents a superb sight as it runs between Billroth and Aich with a train bound for Salzburg in September 1956. The fact that this splendid railway closed prematurely in 1957, was one of the greatest losses that the narrow gauge lines of Europe suffered during the years following World War 2. (P. Hay)*

3.10 *0-10-0TT no.22 was photographed at Lueg, on the shore of the* **Wolfgangsee,** *with a train from Salzburg in September 1956. The ferry from St.Gilgen to St.Wolfgang can be seen on the lake. (P. Hay)*

3.11 *No.3 passes the timber yard at Zinkenbach whilst en route to Salzburg in September 1956. Timber from this source had provided regular freight traffic, although by the time of this photograph much of the output was despatched by road. (P. Hay)*

3.12   Nearing the end of its active career, 0-6-2T no.4 was viewed at Strobl with a train from Salzburg in September 1956. Fortunately, this early example of Austrian narrow gauge locomotive design has survived. Following many years on a plinth at Pfandl, it is now part of the SKGLB museum collection at Mondsee. (P. Hay)

3.13   0-6-2T no.3 and 0-10-0TT no.22 were seen double heading a heavy train from Bad Ischl to Salzburg, at Pfandl on 16th September 1956. A door on the second carriage appears to be open! (P. Hay)

3.14   Borsig 0-10-0TT no.22 stands at Bad Ischl station on 16th September 1956, about to depart for Salzburg. It is difficult to believe, when looking at these historic photographs, that the SKGLB was due to close 12 months later. (P. Hay)

4. STEIERMÄRKISCHE LANDESBAHNEN

The province of Styria in South Eastern Austria lies mainly in the foothills of the eastern extremity of the Alpine mountain chain. It also boasts the most extensive independent railway system in Austria. Originally built and operated by the provincial government, the Styrian Local Government Railway or *Steiermärkische Landesbahnen* (StLB) embraced a network of both standard gauge and 76cm narrow gauge routes. Although officially under the control of the province, the railway system is operated by an independent company with its headquarters at Graz.

The five 76cm lines, of which four have survived, were opened between 1892 and 1930. The five lines ran between Unzmarkt and Maunterndorf (76 km), Weiz and Birkfeld (24 km) with an 18 km extension to Ratten, Kapfenberg to Au-Seewiesen (23 km), Stainz to Preding (12 km) and Mixnitz to St.Erhard (11km). Of these, only the Unzmarkt line, known as the *Murtalbahn,* still operates a regular passenger service. Even that has been cut back to Tamsweg, the final 12 km to Mauterndorf having closed in 1980.

The Weiz to Birkfeld line opened in 1911 and was closed to passengers in 1973, but remained open for freight traffic. Its main usage currently is for the haulage of talcum traffic from Oberfeistritz and steam hauled tourist trains during the summer months. The extension to Ratten, opened in 1930 to serve the coal mines in that area, closed during 1980 after the mines ceased production.

The Kapfenberg line dating from 1893, although ceasing to carry passengers in 1959, still operated a limited freight service from Kapfenberg to Seebach-Turnau until 2000. During the days of steam operation, the line was home to three Z Class 0-6-0Ts. These were supplemented after WW 2 by several larger locomotives including Kh Class 0-10-0T no. Kh 101 and a HF 110 Class 0-6-0TT no.11805, built for the German *Heeresfeldbahn* by B.M.F. Currently in store at Kapfenberg is the unique and nomadic no.Bh 1. This was the prototype of the superheated Uh Class and previously ran on many of the State owned lines, where it was numbered 398.01.

The oldest of the group, the short line at Stainz opened in 1892 and was another victim of rationalisation with passenger services being terminated in 1932, whilst freight services continued until 1980. After the line closed it was leased by the local community for the operation of a limited steam hauled tourist service between Stainz and Preding, using former SKGLB 0-6-2T no. S 11 to provide the motive power. Currently a Romanian 0-8-0T, no. 764.411, is in use on the line whilst the 0-6-2T is undergoing an overhaul. Interestingly, one of the former regular locomotives on the *Stainzerbahn,* a HF 110 Class 0-6-0TT no.11810 built by Jung for the German *Heeresfeldbahn* in 1944, was sold to France in 1970. Following restoration and re-gauging to 70cm, it now works on the *Chemin de Fer d'Abreschviller* in Alsace (see *Northern France Narrow Gauge*).

The Mixnitz to St. Erhard line opened in 1913 using electric locomotives running off a 600 volts overhead supply (later modified to 800 volts). The primary function of the line was to serve the magnasite works at St.Erhard – which it continues to do. A passenger service was also provided, although this ceased to run in 1966. The original two axle electric locomotives, nos E1 and E2, built by AEG in 1913 are still in service. These were joined by two BoBo machines, nos E3 and E4 from ÖAMG in 1957 and 1963.

The Murtalbahn

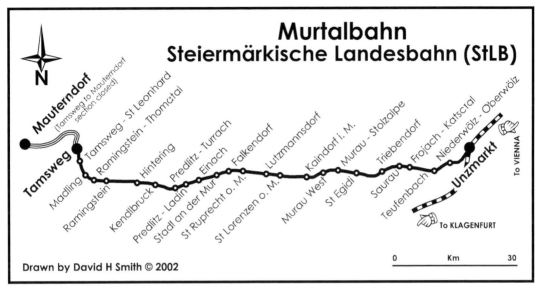

Drawn by David H Smith © 2002

This StLB 76cm line opened on 8th October 1894 between Unzmarkt, on the main Semmering route between Vienna and Klagenfurt, and Mauterndorf in the shadow of the Tauern Alps. Its principal function was that of a local branch line serving the many communities along the 76km route. Although remaining in the valley floor for much of the route, some obstacles had to be overcome necessitating the construction of three tunnels and five large bridges along with some steep gradients. Although operated by the Styrian province, the upper terminus was in the neighbouring province of Salzburgland. The principal intermediate stations were at Frojach-Katschtal, Murau-Stolzalpe, Ramingstein and Tamsweg. Following the rationalisation of Austrian local transport during the 1980s, the final 12km at the western end of the line between Tamsweg and Mauterndorf was closed, thus eliminating the section in the province of Salzburgland. The main depot and workshops are located at Murau-Stolzalpe, which is also the administrative centre of the *Murtalbahn.*

During the years of steam operation, the line was synonymous with the ubiquitous U Class locomotives. These were invariably fitted with the spark arresting devices to their chimneys, in view of the many areas of dense woodland along the route. In 1926 the 0-6-2Ts were joined by no.Kh 101, one of the impressive superheated 0-10-0Ts built at Linz. Another of these powerful machines, no.Kh 111, was transferred from Weiz to Murau in 1943. These locomotives were acquired principally for freight haulage, but were equally used at the head of passenger trains, which often ran as mixed trains.

Diesel power made its first appearance on the *Murtalbahn* in 1933 when three Austro-Daimler diesel railcars entered service. Since 1964, traffic has been in the hands of seven BoBo diesel Electric locomotives and a number of two-car railcar sets, the first of which arrived in 1980. However, the steam locomotives have not been forgotten and three 0-6-2Ts have been retained for regular steam hauled services that operate between June and September, mainly on Tuesdays, Wednesdays and Saturdays. These include U Class nos U 11, U 40 and U 43. Also preserved at Murau is a locomotive that originally worked on the Stainz line. This is no. St 2, a small 0-4-0T built at Linz in 1892.

The "Club 760" has an extensive museum at Frojach with a large collection of motive power. The majority of these are of Austrian origin, plus a number from elsewhere including Yugoslavia and Germany. Many of the locomotives are in working order and are regularly used on special trains in co-operation with the StLB. These include weekend forays along the closed section of line between Tamsweg and Mauterndorf, which is now operated by a separate concern known as the *Taurachbahn Gmbh.* In addition, locomotives from the collection are often loaned to other railways, such as the Yugoslavian 0-8-2 that has been working on the *Zillertalbahn* since 1994. Locomotives of Austrian origin in the Frojach collection include 0-6-2Ts S 7 and 298.56, 0-10-0T no.Kh 111 and 0-6-0T Z 6. One of the Franco-Belge 0-8-0TTs, no. 699.01 is also preserved along with many industrial locomotives. In addition two more locomotives from the former Yugoslavia, 73 Class 2-6-2 no.73.019 and 97 Class 0-6-4 no. 97.029 plus a Romanian 0-8-0T no.764.219 are included in the collection.

**4.1   Steiermärkische Landesbahnen *Z Class 0-6-0T no.6, was viewed at Kapfenberg on 9th September 1958. Note the improvised coal bunker on top of the water tank. Forward visibility for the fireman was obviously considered to be less important than the fuel capacity!*
*(D. Trevor Rowe)***

4.2   *0-6-2T no. U 44 prepares to depart from Kapfenberg with a short mixed train in June 1959. This is one of the later U Class locomotives, with a rear coal bunker. It is also one of the many preserved narrow gauge locomotives in Austria, and now works on the* **Feistritztalbahn** *between Weiz and Birkfeld. (K. Taylorson coll.)*

4.3   *An immaculate 0-6-2T no. U 40 arrives at Unzmarkt, where a connection is made with the Semmering route of the ÖBB, hauling a* **Murtalbahn** *train from Maunterndorf on 13th September 1958. This was one of five U class locomotives that were built at Wiener Neustadt in 1908. (D. Trevor Rowe).*

4.4 *Fitted with a small snow plough, no.U 43 departs from Ramingstein with a train from Unzmarkt to Maunterndorf in February 1963. In common with all alpine railways, snow wasn't considered to be a hazard that would curtail the timetable. (M. Dahlström – J.K.Williams coll.)*

4.5 *0-10-0T no. Kh 111 attacks an incline near Ramingstein in September 1956. This was one of three similar locomotives built between 1924 and 1930, two of which were supplied to the StLB. This was the last one, delivered in 1930, which differed from the earlier versions in being fitted with Caprotti valve gear. (P. Hay)*

4.6   No. Kh 111 presents a splendid sight as it storms away from Ramingstein on the same occasion, en route to Tamsweg and Mauterndorf. (P. Hay)

4.7   0-6-2T no. U 9 is seen at Mauterndorf with a lightweight freight train in September 1956. Like all the U Class locomotives that operated on the StLB, U 9 is fitted with a characteristic spark- arresting chimney. (P. Hay)

4.8   An evening train prepares to depart from Mauterndorf to Unzmarkt hauled by no. Kh 111. Although intended primarily for freight duties, the 0-10-0Ts were often employed on passenger trains, as in this case on 12th September 1958. (D. Trevor Rowe)

The Feistritztalbahn

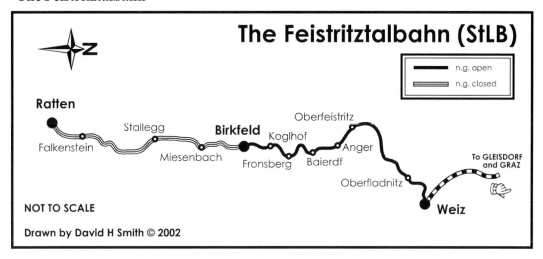

The line from Weiz to Birkfeld follows the Feistritz valley for much of its 24km route. With steep gradients and a succession of tunnels and viaducts, this is one of the most scenic narrow gauge lines in Austria. Opened in 1911, it connected the valley communities with the standard gauge StLB route between Weiz and Gleisdorf. At Gleisdorf a connection was made with the State system.

In 1930, the line was extended a further 18km to the mining village of Ratten. This relatively short-lived section which closed in the 1980, was principally a freight line. The once daily passenger train was provided mainly for the conveyance of mine workers, the locomotive and rolling stock remaining stabled at the upper terminus during the working day.

The journey from Weiz to Ratten was one of undulating variety. Climbing out of Weiz in a north-eastern direction, the line crossed several small valleys before negotiating a hairpin curve leading to a 300 metre long viaduct at Grub. Almost immediately after the viaduct was crossed, a tunnel was negotiated, after which another viaduct spanning the Feistritz valley was traversed. Finally yet another tunnel led to the first summit of the line, before a steep twisting descent to the intermediate station at Anger. There then followed a steep climb in a northerly direction through a densely forested area, via two more tunnels and a precipitous ledge on the hillside near Koglhof, before descending to Birkfeld.

The extension to Ratten was through another area of forests and rushing torrents of the upper reaches of the Feistritz valley. As was so often the case, Ratten was a mining settlement set amidst beautiful scenery. Since the closure of the mines 30 years ago, the reminders of its industrial past have been swept away and the area has become a favourite venue for a variety of outdoor pursuits.

Like the *Murtalbahn*, the *Feistritzalbahn* relied on the ubiquitous U Class 0-6-2Ts for the majority of its motive power requirements. As with the similar locomotives that worked between Unzmarkt and Mauterndorf, the members of the U Class were fitted with the characteristic spark arresting devices. In 1930, the last of the 0-10-0Ts, no. Kh 111, was acquired with the possibility of heavy coal traffic from Ratten. No. Kh 111 was transferred to the Murtalbahn in 1943, whilst in 1980 the other StLB 0-10-0T, no. Kh 101, was transferred from Kapfenberg, where it had been based since 1965. In 1956, no. U 38 was the subject of an experiment when it was fitted with a Giesl Ejector, the only member of the U Class to be so treated. The results were very impressive with a marked increase in power and fuel economy. However, U 38's life in its modified form was to be short lived. In August 1962, it ran into a landslide near Koglhof and was badly damaged. Consequently it was withdrawn from service and cannibalised for spare parts. As steam traction in regular service was drawing to an end, it was decided not to proceed further with the Giesl experiments.

Following the closure of the SKGLB in 1957, the opportunity was taken to acquire additional locomotives. Thus three 0-6-2Ts, nos S 7, S 11 and S 12 were transferred along with Franco-Belge KDL 11 type 0-8-0TT no.19. The latter was rebuilt as a 0-8-0T and worked regularly on the line until 1969 when it was offered for sale. As a result, the locomotive came to Great Britain, being purchased by the Welshpool and Llanfair Railway. Since 1970, *Sir Drefaldwyn* as it was named after purchase, has been a constant and reliable performer on the Welsh line. During the period it was working on the StLB this locomotive was renumbered 699.01, which was to cause some confusion as the ÖBB also had a Franco-Belge 0-8-0TT numbered 699.01. The latter has also survived into preservation, being part of the "Club 760" collection at Frojach.

Diesel power in the shape of BoBo DE locomotives took over the regular services during the 1960s, whilst the steam locomotives were retained for "special occasions". Passenger services ceased in 1973 and the Weiz to Birkfeld line continued as a freight only operation.

The scenic attraction of the *Feistritztalbahn,* was not to be ignored by the energetic StLB management, following the end of regular passenger services. Consequently some of the steam locomotives were retained for hauling tourist trains between June and October. These run mainly on Mondays, Wednesdays, Thursdays and Sundays. Currently based at Weiz, are 0-10-0T no.Kh 101, 0-6-2Ts nos. U8 and U44 and a Yugoslavian 83 class 0-8-2 no. 83.180. The latter is owned by a supporting group known, as "Club U44", which also has a small museum in the engine shed at Birkfeld, where another 0-6-2T no. U7 is on display. The steam hauled trains operate between Weiz and Birkfeld, and are run by the StLB, in conjunction with the Weiz Tourist Board and "Club U44". It is a combined operation that works well and the sight and sound of the powerful 0-10-0T climbing the steep gradients of the *Feistritztalbahn* is one of lasting memory.

4.9   Franco-Belge type KDL 11 0-8-0T no. 699.01 was seen at Weiz, on the **Feistritztalbahn** *section of the StLB. The mixed train had just arrived from Birkfeld on 10th September 1958. This locomotive was formerly no.19 on the SKGLB, where it ran as a 0-8-0TT. In 1970 it was sold to the Welshpool and Llanfair Railway where it now operates as their no.10, named "Sir Drefaldwyn". (D. Trevor Rowe)*

4.10   Former SKGLB 0-6-2T no. S 12 was photographed at Anger, with a Weiz to Birkfeld train, on 10th September 1958. This was the last of the "S Class" locomotives built at Linz, being delivered in 1906. It differed from the other members of the class in being fitted with a rear bunker. (D. Trevor Rowe)

4.11   On the same date, no. S 12 was viewed shunting the stock of a mixed train at Birkfeld. By that period, the majority of trains terminated there, the extension to Ratten being used very little. (D. Trevor Rowe)

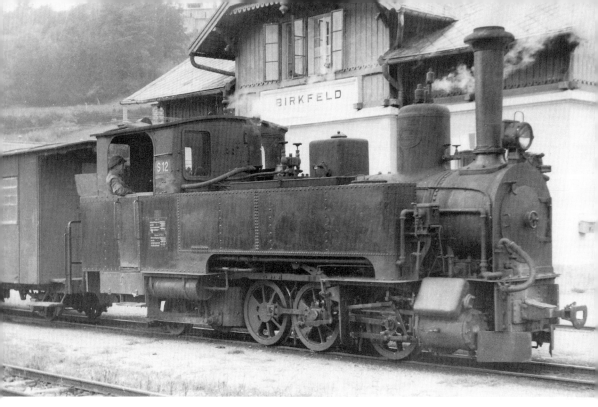

4.12   The driver of no. S 12 rests between shunting operations at Birkfeld on 10th September 1958. There was probably no urgency to complete the job! (D. Trevor Rowe)

4.13   A later view of 0-6-2T no. S 12 shows it standing alongside the goods shed at Birkfeld. By the time of this undated photograph, the locomotive had been overhauled and modified, which included the fitting of full-length U Class side tanks, possibly from the withdrawn U 38. (K. Taylorson coll.)

4.14   0-10-0T no. Kh 101 climbs up the gradient from Weiz with a tourist train bound for Birkfeld on 5th August 1993. Unlike its younger sister locomotive no. Kh 111, this machine is fitted with conventional piston valves and motion. (Miss S. Benn)

4.15   Shortly after a heavy thunderstorm, during which the temperature dropped 16 degrees centigrade in 30 minutes, 0-10-0T no. Kh 101 is seen leaving Anger en route for Birkfeld during the late afternoon of 5th August 1993. (Miss S. Benn)

5. THE ÖBB RACK AND PINION LINES

Of the three metre gauge mountain rack railways in Austria, two are part of the ÖBB network, although one of those was originally part of an independent operation. The two lines are the *Schafbergbahn*, south of Salzburg and the *Schneebergbahn*, located to the south of Vienna. Both use identical locomotives and rolling stock and were opened within three years of each other. However, although they are both now very much part of the tourist scene, the original aims of the *Schneebergbahn* were quite different. Whilst the earlier line near Salzburg is located in the Alpine region of mountains and lakes, the later line climbs the very eastern extremity of the Alpine chain in an area that was not embraced into the tourist circuit until more recent times.

The Schafbergbahn

Originally part of the *Salzkammergut-Lokalbahn* undertaking, the 6km Abt system rack and pinion line from St.Wolfgang to the summit of the Schafberg opened in 1893. From the lakeside lower terminus to the 1783 metre summit, the railway climbs 1500 metres at an average gradient of 1in 5. The reason for its construction was purely for transporting tourists to this famous mountain, where unsurpassed views of the surrounding mountains and lakes can be seen from the summit. Like all such mountain top stations, this was developed into a hotel and tourist centre with the usual array of souvenir shops and other attractions.

The lower terminus on the shores of the *Wolfgangsee* was also famous in its own right. Regarded as one of the most picturesque lakeside villages in the Alps, it was also the home of the famous "White Horse Inn" which had given its name to an Operetta of the same name.

Following the annexation of Austria into Germany in 1938, the Austrian State railway system was absorbed into the German network, *Deutsche Reichsbahn* (DRB). With the Austrian Alps now part of an enlarged Germany, their attraction was quickly sought as a destination for holidays and visits away from the major cities during that difficult period. In an attempt to attract more custom, the DRB took over the *Schafbergbahn* from the SKGLB, which was unable to cope with the many extra visitors to the area.

Following the end of hostilities and Austria regaining its independence, the *Schafbergbahn* remained under state control, being now part of the ÖBB network. Following the demise of the SKGLB, and its ferry link across the lake, the mountain railway has continued to provide a regular service to the summit during the summer months. Capital investment has included the purchase of diesel powered rail cars to take some of the increasing workload from the original steam locomotives, whilst new locomotives built in Switzerland were delivered during the last decade.

The journey up the line is similar to many other mountain rack and pinion lines. With the steep ascent beginning immediately after departure from the station area, the initial climb is through woodland with the occasional chalet among the clearings. Once above the tree line, the line winds its way around the mountain before emerging at the upper station, a short distance below the summit. There are no notable civil engineering structures such as tunnels and viaducts, but the views from the train as it makes its relentless climb are quite magnificent.

The Schneebergbahn

Opened in 1896 by the Imperial-Royal Austrian State Railways, the 10km Abt system metre gauge line from Puchberg to Hochschneeberg was built originally to provide a daily service for the communities among the wooded slopes of the Schneeberg. Although tourism is now the major source of income, the railway still provides a daily year round service to the 1795 metre summit, which is the highest station in Austria. In addition to passenger traffic, some limited freight trains are also operated, much of it destined for the small settlement at Hochschneeberg. During the climb from the

577m.lower terminus, where there is a connection with a standard gauge branch line, the lines ascends 1200 metres at an average gradient of 1 in 9 and a maximum of 1 in 5.

Although not in a well known tourist area, the railway has become well patronised since WW 2 due, no doubt, to its easy accessibility from Vienna and other major centres. Although the summit lacks the supreme views of other mountains, Hochschneeberg boasts a number of walks and the usual gift shops and restaurant, plus a large church with quite magnificent stained glass windows.

The ÖBB managed to keep the original locomotives working, without the need to resort to diesel power for additional capacity, until the end of the 20th Century. In order to cope with increased traffic, one of the identical locomotives from the *Schafbergbahn* was transferred some years ago, whilst additional new Swiss built locomotives were delivered during the 1990s. However some two-car diesel units were delivered during 2000 which currently operate many of the services.

The journey from Puchberg is mainly through woodland, passing a number of small hamlets during the climb. About half way along the ascent is the major intermediate station on a hillside ledge. This incorporates a passing loop and watering facilities. The final section, above the tree line, climbs around the rocky upper reaches of the mountain before terminating at the spacious station in the centre of the mountain top village.

The ÖBB rack and pinion locomotives

Both railways took delivery of identical locomotives, built by Krauss Linz, between 1893 and 1900.

Six were supplied to the Schafberg line in 1893-94 and ultimately received the ÖBB classification of 999.1, numbered 999.101 – 106. Four more were supplied to the Schneeberg operation between 1896 and 1900. These were classified as 999.0 and numbered 999.01 – 04. The locomotives were powerful 0-4-2RTs with a weight in working order of 18 tonnes. The two 320 x 600mm cylinders were placed midway above the coupled wheels. The piston rod was facing forward, driving a vertical oscillating link from which the rack pinions were powered.

The major modification to these locomotives occurred during the late 1950s, when they were fitted with Giesl Ejectors in place of their original stovepipe chimneys. The increase in power and fuel economy afforded by these modifications undoubtedly increased the active life of these venerable machines.

With increased traffic on both lines, measures had to be taken during the 1960s to maintain the service. Two diesel railcars appeared at St.Wolfgang in 1964 whilst no. 999.101was transferred to Puchberg. However the diesels proved to be unpopular, with many passengers waiting at the lower terminus for the next steam-propelled train.

The situation was resolved in 1988 when the *Schweizerische Lokomotiv und Maschinenfabrik* (SLM) at Winterthur, Switzerland, introduced a new design of a revolutionary oil fired rack and pinion locomotive. Incorporating latest technology alongside traditional features, these splendid machines were also designed for one-man operation. The original prototypes were supplied to the 80cm *Brienz-Rothorn-Bahn* in Switzerland, where the power and efficiency of these modern locomotives was proved. The design had allowed them to be built in a variety of gauges, the result being that the ÖBB have acquired six metre gauge examples since 1992. Four are now at work on the *Schafbergbahn* with the other two on the *Schneebergbahn.* These 0-4-2RTs are designated as the 999.2 class, nos 999.201-204 being based at St.Wolfgang and 999.205-6 at Puchberg.

The older Linz built locomotives were able to propel two carriages on the Schneeberg line, but were limited to one vehicle on the steeper Schafberg route. This obviously created problems at busy periods, and was a major factor in acquiring the railcars. However, the SLM locomotives are able to propel two heavily laden carriages with ease. As a result, the original Schafberg locomotives are in semi-retirement, their use being confined to special occasions. On the Schneeberg, the venerable machines from Linz work alongside their younger Swiss cousins, although the latter are not surprisingly handling the majority of the traffic.

St.Wolfgang is easily reached from Salzburg or Bad Ischl by bus, whilst Puchberg enjoys a good rail service from Vienna (Wien Südbahnhof), via Wiener Neustadt. Being part of the state railway system, they are relatively cheap to travel on. Unlike some of the privately operated mountain railways in other countries, they are not subjected to high supplements and correspondingly expensive fares.

5.1   Krauss 0-4-2RT no. 999.106 is seen leaving St. Wolfgang and immediately begins the steep climb to the Schafberg summit, in September 1990. The chalets overlooking the line at this point offer a grandstand view of the railway. (J.F. Organ)

5.2   An excellent view of the lower section of the route is visible as no. 999.106 continues the relentless climb on the same occasion. The Abt system rack and pinion track can be seen between the running rails. (J.F. Organ)

5.3   This is one of the SLM locomotives supplied in 1992. No.999.201 is seen arriving at St. Wolfgang on 21ˢᵗ May 2001. The immaculate condition of the station is clearly seen in this photograph. (J.A. Foster).

5.4 *The oil fired, single manned, locomotive waits at St. Wolfgang before making another ascent of the 6 km line to the summit. These highly efficient machines, incorporating much modern technology, have revolutionised the operation of mountain railways in both Austria and Switzerland. (J.A. Foster)*

5.5 *Sister locomotive no. 999.203 prepares to depart from St. Wolfgang on the same occasion. Unlike the earlier locomotives, the SLM machines are not fitted with Giesel Ejectors. (J.A. Foster)*

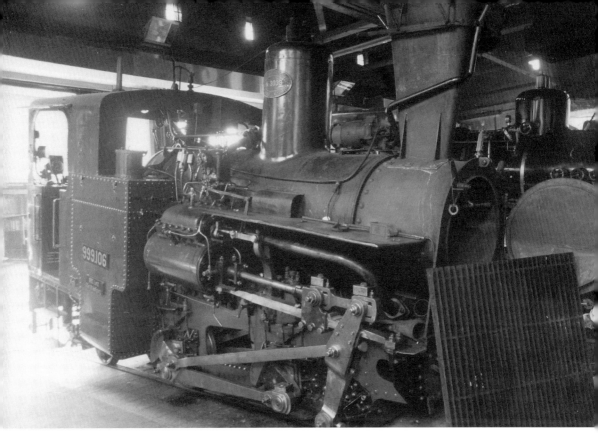

5.6   One of the original **Schafbergbahn** *locomotives, no. 999.106, dating from 1894, was receiving attention in the workshops at St. Wolfgang. The high mounted cylinder and valve gear can be seen to good effect in this view. (J.A. Foster)*

5.7   *The clean uncluttered lines of the SLM locomotives are a complete contrast to the vintage machines from Linz. No.999.204 was seen undergoing maintenance to its motion on 21ˢᵗ May 2001. (J.A.Foster)*

5.8   No. 999.101, carrying its former DRB number 997306, ascends the higher reaches of the climb. This undated view shows the locomotive before it was fitted with a Giesel Ejector. (J.K.Williams coll.)

5.9   The Schafberg summit, as no. 999.103 was seen climbing towards the upper station on 23rd June 1970. The large hotel complex, with its commanding views, is very prominent above the station. (J.K.Williams coll.)

5.10   This is the depot at Puchberg, the lower terminus of the **Schneebergbahn**, *where two of the original Krauss built 0-4-2RTs were photographed being prepared for their duties. At this time in September 1990, these vintage locomotives were the only motive power, they were due to be joined by a pair of the new SLM machines two years later. (J.F. Organ)*

5.11   *"Kneeling cow" at rest. No.999.03 was receiving attention outside the engine shed at Puchberg, before propelling a train to the summit, on 10th September 1990. (J.F.Organ)*

5.12. *The passing loop at the intermediate station of the Schneeberg line. Note how the gradient increases sharply beyond the points in the distance, whilst no.999.05 takes water before resuming the ascent to Hochschneeberg. (J.F. Organ)*

5.13   *The summit at Hochschneeberg is partly shrouded in mist, as two of the 0-4-2RTs stand in the station on 10th September 1990. No.999.01 has arrived with a passenger train whilst former Schafberg locomotive no.999.101 is in charge of a train of tank wagons. Note the spark arresting devices hinged in the open position on the Giesel Ejectors. (J.F. Organ)*

6. ALPINE BORDERS

The majority of the railways featured in this publication have been located in the vicinity of the Alpine regions of Austria. There were also many other narrow gauge railways, worthy of consideration, which operated away from the mountainous regions. Without exception, these ultimately became part of the ÖBB network despite retaining their original names. Some were closed during the rationalisation of the 1970s, whilst others have become casualties of more recent closures. Time is also running out for some of the surviving lines as a result of the ÖBB being under pressure from central government to close its unprofitable minor routes, no doubt to be replaced by buses. In all probability, some of these "doomed" lines may be acquired by the private sector. The Zell am See to Krimml line, described in Chapter Two, falls into this category and two of the principal independent railway companies have expressed an interest. Sections of other lines, already closed, have been transformed into successful museum lines. Despite limited operating periods, the preservation scene in Austria is almost as strong as in Great Britain.

Steyrtalbahn

Opened between 1889 and 1891, the *Steyrtalbahn,* south of Linz, was one of the first 76cm railways to be constructed following the *Lokalbahn Legislation* of 1887. The 40km line ran from a northern terminus at Garsten to Klaus, both termini connecting with major standard gauge routes, plus a 15km branch from Pergern to Bad Hall. Intermediate stations along this scenic line through the valley of the River Steyr were located at Steyr, Pergern, Aschach, Grünburg, Molln and Leonstein.

Steam reigned supreme on the *Steyrtalbahn* until its closure in 1982. The reason for diesel motive power not being supplied to replace the ageing steam locomotives was due to an impending road improvement scheme through the valley, which forced the ÖBB to close the line prematurely. Consequently, a fleet of hardy 0-6-2Ts worked the line until the end. The first locomotives were the original batch of *"Steyrtalbahn Loks",* later numbered in the 298.101 series, whilst for the majority of its life, the ubiquitous U Class locomotives of the 298.01 series were synonymous with the line.

In addition to a regular passenger service, extensive freight was also carried on the line. Much of this was timber from the large sawmills near Steyr. With main line connections at each end of the route, onward transportation of freight throughout the country was easily achieved.

The above mentioned road improvement scheme affected the southern section of the line. Following closure in 1982, a preservation group based at Linz, known as *Österreichischen Gesellschaft für Eisenbahngeschichte* or Austrian Society for Railway History (ÖGEG) secured the use of the northern section of the route between Steyr and Grünburg. Depots were created at Grünburg and Steyr where a number of the original locomotives and items of rolling stock were restored to a high standard. Among the collection are U Class nos 298.52 and 298.53, "S Class" nos 298.102 and 298.106, Uh Class 498.04 and 498.06 and Franco-Belge 0-8-0T 699.103. In addition to the Austrian machines, a Romanian 0-8-0T no. 764.007 also works on the *Steyrtalbahn.*

Running at weekends during the summer months between May and September, the ÖGEG operation is one of the most authentic reminders of the Austrian 76cm lines in their prime. Normally three return journeys are made during each day's operation, with additional trains often added at peak periods. Steyr is easily accessible from Linz by rail or road.

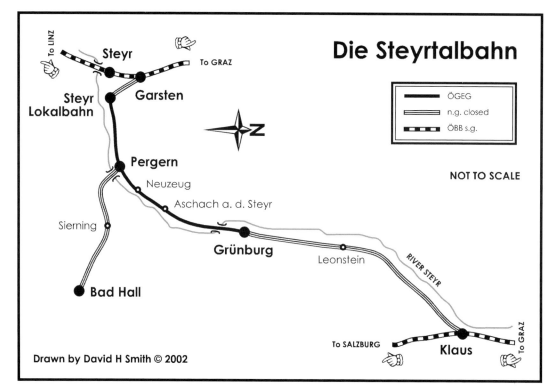

6.1   A general view of Garsten shed, the principal depot of the Steyrtalbahn. Four U Class 0-6-2Ts were photographed in this busy scene on 2nd June 1974. Seen left to right are nos 298.56, 298.53, 298.51 and 298.52. (J.K. Williams)

6.2 *U Class no. 298.53 and Steyrtalbahn Lok no. 298.104 were captured at Garsten on 24th June 1970. Both locomotives spent all their working lives on the Steyr line, prior to preservation by the ÖGEG and ÖGLB respectively. (J.K. Williams)*

6.3 *Another view of no. 298.53 shows it at Garsten, as it raises steam on 5th September 1958. Note that the U Class locomotives on this ÖBB line were not fitted with spark arresting chimneys. (D.Trevor Rowe)*

6.4   *A final view of Garsten shed includes two U class locomotives, nos 298.53 and 298.25 being prepared for duty on 6th July 1976. The engine shed is as equally attractive as the locomotives. (B. Benn)*

6.5   *U Class no. 298.53 departs from Grünburg, with a freight train from Garsten to Klaus on 7th July 1976. The River Steyr is seen to the right of the photograph. (B. Benn)*

6.6   0-6-2T no. 298.25 was photographed hauling a passenger train between Grünburg and Leonstein on 6th July 1976. The immaculate state of the permanent way is apparent in this view. (B. Benn)

6.7   No. 298.53 is seen again, with a heavy timber train as it crosses the main road near Mölln, en route from Klaus to the sawmills near Steyr, on 7th July 1976. This locomotive is now part of the ÖGEG collection and is still in service on its original line, based at Grünburg. (B. Benn)

6.8   At another level crossing near Grünburg, no.298.52 was photographed with a lightweight southbound passenger train on 6th July 1974. This locomotive is also a member of the ÖGEG collection at Grünburg. (J.K. Williams)

6.9   U Class 0-6-2T no. 298.51 was viewed crossing the River Steyr in a very scenic location near Grünburg on 10th June 1979. Scenes like this were once an everyday occurrence throughout Austria. (J.F. Organ coll.)

6.10   Franco-Belge KDL 11 0-8-0T no. 699.103, of the ÖGEG collection, is seen at work on the Steyrtalbahn museum line. The locomotive was viewed replenishing its coal-bunker at Grünburg in September 1992. (A. Heywood)

Ybbstalbahn

Situated about 20 km east of Steyr is Waidhofen an der Ybbs, on the standard gauge route between Amstetten and Selzthal. It is also the western terminus of a 71km long, 76cm gauge, line that connected with another standard gauge line at Kienberg-Gaming. Known as the *Ybbstalbahn* in view of its close proximity to the River Ybbs, the scenic route had intermediate stations at Hollenstein, Göstling and Lunz am See, in addition to a number of wayside halts. The line also has a 6km branch from Gstadt to Ybbsitz.

Opened in 1896, this most attractive line was home to three unique locomotives. The 0-6-4T compound Yv Class, later numbered 598.01 – 03, were delivered in 1896 and remained synonymous with the *Ybbstalbahn*. They were assisted by some of the U and Uh Class 0-6-2s, whilst prior to 1973 the nomadic prototype Uh, no.398.01, also worked on the line. Since the 1960s, diesel locomotives of the B-B 2095 Class have been responsible for the majority of the haulage, both for passenger and freight, with 5090 Class diesel railcars being introduced from 1995.

In 1989, the 17km section between Kienberg-Gaming and Lunz am See was closed, leaving the 54 km route between Waidhofen and Lunz as the only connection with the main line network. Despite this reduction in route mileage, the surviving section continued to offer a regular limited service. Being a mainly agricultural area, the fairly light freight traffic has been mainly concerned with the farming industry and the inevitable timber haulage, whilst the majority of passenger traffic has primarily been that normally associated with a rural branch line.

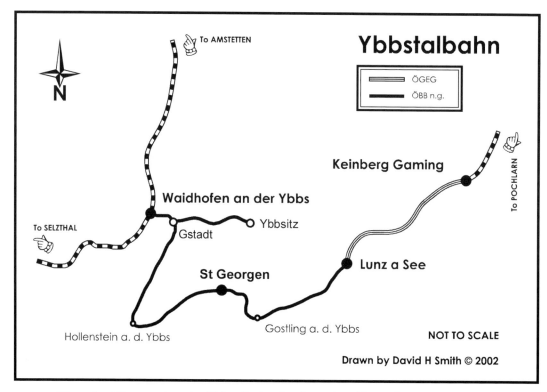

To AMSTETTEN

Ybbstalbahn

ÖGEG
ÖBB n.g.

Keinberg Gaming

To POCHLARN

Waidhofen an der Ybbs

Ybbsitz

To SELZTHAL

Gstadt

Lunz a See

St Georgen

Hollenstein a. d. Ybbs

Gostling a. d. Ybbs

NOT TO SCALE

Drawn by David H Smith © 2002

Steam is still present on the *Ybbstalbahn,* thanks to the efforts of two preservation groups. "Club 598" is based at Waidhofen where it has preserved 0-6-4Ts nos 598.02 and 598.03 since 1973. The former, running as Yv2, has hauled numerous special trains along the line, whilst her sister locomotive is being restored for similar duties. The third member of the class, 598.01, is preserved as a static exhibit in Carinthia.

The other preservation group involved with the *Ybbstalbahn* is the ÖGLB, (Österreichische *Gesellschaft Für Lokalbahnen)* who have leased the closed section of line between Kienberg-Gaming and Lunz am See. Three locomotives from their collection, U Class 298.51, Uv Class 298.205 and *Steyrtalbahn* 298.104, plus a vintage diesel locomotive no. 2093.01 built in 1930, are based at Kienberg-Gaming and are used for weekend services during the summer months. This is probably the most scenic section of the entire route, including two trestle viaducts and steep gradients.

The remaining ÖBB section from Lunz am See to Waidhofen runs mainly alongside the river in the valley floor, but is still very attractive and crosses several spectacular bridges. Regular steam hauled tourist trains also run over this section of the line with Mh class 0-8+4 locomotives no's. 399.02 and 399.03 being used between1997 and 2001. However in 2002 both required major boiler repairs, as a result of which arrangements were made with "Club 598" to use their locomotive no. 598.02 (Yv2).

6.11 *Yv Class 0-6-4T no. 598.01 stands at Waidhofen an der Ybbs on the* Ybbstalbahn, *about to depart for Keinberg-Gaming on 5th September 1958. (D. Trevor Rowe)*

6.12 *Another view of no. 598.01 shows it as it prepares to depart from Waidhofen on the same occasion. The three members of the Yv Class were synonymous with the* Ybbstalbahn, *and all have survived into preservation. (D. Trevor Rowe)*

6.13   *Uh Class 0-6-2T no.498.07 is seen shunting at Waidhofen on 5th September 1958. This is one of the locomotives built at Floridsdorf in 1931, fitted with Lentz Poppet Valve Gear. (D. Trevor Rowe)*

6.14   *Diesel no. 2093.01 pilots Yv Class no.598.03 into Waidhofen in September 1958. Such a combination of motive power was a rare sight on the Austrian narrow gauge network. (D. Trevor Rowe)*

6.15   *A passenger train is seen arriving at the delightful rural station at Waidhofen, hauled by diesel locomotive no. 2091.11 on 5th September 1958. (D. Trevor Rowe)*

6.16   *Uv Class 0-6-2T no. 298.205 arrives at Keinberg-Gaming on 6th September 1958, hauling a train from Waidhofen. Keinberg-Gaming was the eastern terminus of the Ybbstalbahn, where a connection was made with the standard gauge branch from Pöchlarn. (D. Trevor Rowe)*

6.17   *Preserved Yv Class no.598.02 hauls a special charter train from Waidhofen to Lunz am See. It was seen near Hohenlehen on 1ˢᵗ August 1993, where it presented a splendid sight. (Mrs. B. Benn)*

6.18   *On the same date, the 0-6-4T was seen crossing a minor road near Gross Hollenstein. In its preserved condition, the locomotive carries the number Yv2 and is painted green, in place of the black livery in which Austrian locomotives were usually painted. (Miss S. Benn)*

6.19 No. 598.02 (Yv2) presents another superb spectacle as it runs alongside the river at St. Georgen, en route to Lunz am See with the special train on 1st August 1993. (Miss. S. Benn)

6.20 During the return journey to Waidhofen, the Yv Class 0-6-4T drifts downhill from Lunz am See in the late afternoon of 1st August 1993, having been turned on the turntable at the latter station. (Mrs. B. Benn)

6.21   Former Steyrtalbahn *U Class 0-6-2T no.298.51, now running as no.U.1, was photographed as it climbed over the trestle viaduct at Pfaffenschlag with an ÖGLB tourist train from Keinberg-Gaming to Lunz am See on 31ˢᵗ July 1993. (Mrs. B. Benn)*

Mariazellerbahn

St.Pölten, a major junction and railway centre on the Vienna to Salzburg route, is the starting point of the Austrian 76cm line that boasts the steepest gradients, as well as many viaducts and tunnels-the longest of which is 2368 metres long. The 84.2km line runs south to the historic town of Mariazell, which is a major religious and pilgrimage centre. Until 1988, the line ran a further 7km beyond Mariazell to an upper terminus at Guesswek. A regular passenger service has, however, continued to run to Mariazell although freight traffic was withdrawn from the *Mariazellerbahn* on 1st January 1999.

The first section of the line to open in 1898 was the 31km to Kirchberg, using four U Class 0-6-2Ts. The line was fully opened in 1906 when the first of six Mh Class 0-8+4 Engerth locomotives were delivered to haul the trains over the extended route. A further two Mv Class compound 0-8+4s were supplied in 1907. These large powerful locomotives were necessary in view of the steep gradients and severe curvature of the higher section of the route leading to Mariazell, at an altitude of 850m. The initial part of the line is a typical meander along the valley floor. However, after leaving Kirchberg it commences a spectacular climb with long loops and tunnels, more akin to a Swiss mountain railway.

In 1911, the railway was electrified at 6,500 volts AC 25 Hz with a total of sixteen Class 1099 electric locomotives supplied between 1911 and 1914. Rebuilding of these locomotives with new bodywork commenced in 1959 and they are still responsible for hauling much of the traffic on the line today. They were joined by Class 4090 electric multiple units which first appeared in 1997.

The eight steam locomotives delivered between 1906 and 1908 were transferred to the *Waldviertelbahn* following the electrification of the Mariazell line. Nos 399.01 to 399.06 have all survived, the first now working on the Krimml line, whilst the last returned to St.Pölten during the 1950s for use on the Gresten line and occasional special workings to Mariazell. No. 399.06 is now based at Obergrafendorf, whilst the frequency of these steam hauled excursions has increased in recent years. The two compound variants, Mv Class nos 299.01 and 299.02 remained at Obergrafendorf until 1923 when they joined the Mh Engerth's at the *Waldviertelbahn.*

6.22   Engerth Mh Class 0-8+4 no.399.06 was photographed departing from Wieselburg, with a passenger train bound for Gresten on 6th September 1958. A connection with the standard gauge branch from Keinberg-Gaming was made at this station. (D. Trevor Rowe)

6.23   One of the Mv Class compound Engerths, no.299.01 hauls a mixed train on the ÖBB line between Obergrafendorf and Gresten during the 1960s. The two Mv Class locomotives were returned to Obergrafendorf, from Gmünd, in 1961. Both were withdrawn within a short time, 299.01 in 1965 and 299.02 in 1962. They were ultimately used as a basis for snowploughs, following many years in store at Knittelfeld Works. (J.K.Williams coll.)

Obergrafendorf to Gresten

12 km after leaving St.Pölten on the Mariazell line, the first major station is at Obergrafendorf. A junction was created here with a 62.5km line, heading west towards Gresten. A connection was made with the standard gauge branch from Kienberg- Gaming to Pöcklarn at Wieselburg, where the two lines crossed. Originally opened from Obergrafendorf to Ruprechtshofen, the line was extended to Gresten in 1927. In conjunction with this extension, three P Class 0-8-2Ts were delivered, being joined in 1931 by the last of the Floridsdorf built Uh Class 0-6-2Ts. These additional locomotives worked alongside the original motive power, including the two Mv Class Engerth 0-8+4s, which after a long absence returned to the line in 1961.

The Gresten line wasn't electrified, unlike its adjoining line, and never had a busy passenger service. The section of line from Wieselburg to Gresten was closed to passenger traffic on 1st January 1991and the last narrow gauge freight train departed from Gresten on 3rd April 1998, appropriately hauled by Mh Class locomotive no. 399.06. However, the closure of the Wieselburg to Gresten section was due to an increase in freight traffic rather than a decline, the line being converted to standard gauge as a consequence and re-opening in that form on 27th November 1998.

All traffic has been withdrawn between Ruprechtshofen and Wieselburg, the last passenger train running on 15th January 2000. The line remained open between Obergrafendorf and Ruprechtshofen for a limited passenger service but was threatened with closure during 2003. A preservation group known as *Eisenbahnklub Mh6* is based at the locomotive depot at Obergrafendorf. In their care are Mh Class no. 399.06 (running as Mh6), U Class no. 298.54, Uv Class no. 298.207 and diesel locomotives 2091.11, 2190.03 and 2092.03. The 0-8+4 has seen frequent use in recent years hauling special trains to Ruprechtshofen and, as previously mentioned, to Mariazell.

6.24   Although the 0-8+4   Engerth locomotives were originally supplied for use on the **Mariazellerbahn** *in 1906, their life on that line was short, due to it being electrified in 1911. One of the original electric locomotives was seen on the upper reaches of the line in 1914.* **(K.Taylorson coll.)**

6.25   The original electric locomotives are still in service, having been extensively rebuilt with new bodywork during the 1960s. Nos 1099.014 and 1099.013 prepare to depart from Mariazell before double heading a train to St. Pölten on 15th April 1998. (D. Trevor Rowe)

6.26   Engerth 0-8+4 no.399.05 waits at Weitra on the Waldviertelbahn, between Gmünd and Gross Gerungs, in June 1983. These powerful locomotives were usually employed on heavy freight trains, rather than lightweight passenger trains. (R. Todt / BVA)

Waldviertelbahn

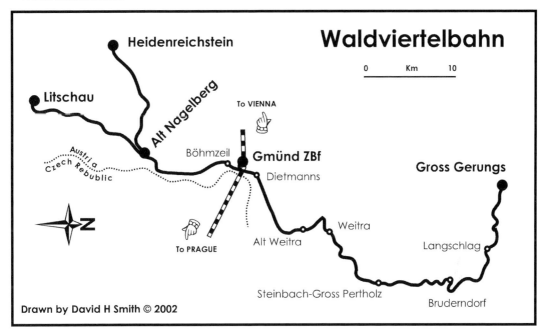

Drawn by David H Smith © 2002

In the north of Austria, close to the Czech border, is the frontier station at Gmünd on the main line between Vienna and Prague. Gmünd was also the hub of an extensive 76cm system known as the *Waldviertelbahn.* Constructed by the Lower Austrian Provincial Railways, later to become part of the ÖBB, the first section was opened in 1900. This was a 25km line running north from Gmünd to Litschau, which ran alongside the border for much of its route. A junction was created at Alt Nagelberg, from where a 13km branch to Heidenreichstein headed in an easterly direction.

During 1902 and 1903, a 43km southern extension was constructed between Gmünd and Gross Gerungs. This twisting and steeply graded line through the densely wooded hills of this thinly populated area of Austria was to earn its place in railway history as being the "last bastion of steam" on a daily basis in the country.

In view of the steep gradients, and the heavy freight traffic generated by the timber industry, the *Waldviertelbahn* was to become synonymous with the Engerth type Mh Class 0-8+4s, which were transferred from St.Pölten in 1911 after the *Mariazellerbahn* was electrified. In later years, much of the freight traffic was conveyed in standard gauge wagons carried precariously on narrow gauge transporter vehicles. The sight and sound of one of the 0-8+4s hauling a load of five fully laden "piggy back" wagons was one that drew enthusiasts to this area from far and wide during the 1970s and 1980s. After the two northern branches were closed to passengers in 1986, and the simultaneous introduction of railcars on the Gross Gerungs line, the steam locomotives were largely retained for these heavy freight workings.

Although diesel locomotives first appeared on the line after the 1960s, four of the Mh Engerths (399.02 – 399.05) and Uv Class 0-6-2T no.298.207 remained. In addition to the freight haulage, they were also in huge demand for the regular special charter trains that seemed to be an everyday occurrence. The majority of these were, not surprisingly, operated on the more scenic southern section of the system. However, the northern lines also had their own particular charm, notably the parallel departures from Alt Nagelberg. Nos 399.02 and 399.03 were transferred to Waidhofen in 1997, whilst no.298.207 is now at Obergrafendorf.

As previously mentioned, the ÖBB has been under government pressure to close its uneconomic branch lines. Not surprisingly, the *Waldviertelbahn* fell into that category and duly closed on 9th June 2001, just 12 months after celebrating its centenary. However, the future of the remaining locomotives should be secure as one of the established preservation groups is hoping to save the Gross Gerungs line. No. 399.04 has been retained in working order at Gmünd for these duties, whilst sister locomotives 399.02 and 399.03 have now returned from Waidhofen and are currently in store. In addition, no.399.05, which is privately owned, is awaiting restoration at Heidenreichstein. The working locomotive has hauled a number of special excursions along the line since it was closed, promoted by a local syndicate. Hopefully these will continue in the future.

6.27   No. 399.05 is seen replenishing its tender at Bruderndorf, with a train from Gross Gerungs in June 1983. The rather primitive water supply system appears to waste almost as much as it supplies! (R. Todt / BVA)

6.28   Sister locomotive no. 399.03 passes the level crossing at Böhmzeil, near Gmünd, on the northern part of the **Walviertelbahn** in May 1983. (R. Todt /BVA)

6.29   Mh Class 0-8+4Ts nos 399.03 and 399.05 were seen at Alt Nagelberg, close to the Czech border, in May 1983. For a short distance north of this station, the two branches to Litschau and Heidenreichstein ran parallel to each other, before heading in their separate directions. (R. Todt/BVA)

6.30   Engerth no. 399.01, now based on the Krimml line, was captured near Alt Nagelberg in May 1983 whilst hauling a passenger train. (R. Todt/BVA)

6.31   Deep in the forests on the branch to Heidenreichstein, no.399.05 was employed on a lightweight mixed train in May 1983. This locomotive is now privately owned and is currently in store at the upper terminus of this rural branch line. (R. Todt/BVA)

6.32   No.399.05 was photographed whilst engaged in shunting operations at Litschau, with two standard gauge hopper wagons precariously mounted on narrow gauge transporter vehicles in May 1983. (R. Todt/BVA)

Narrow Gauge in Carinthia

The province of Carinthia in the south of Austria, near the Slovenia border, was home to two 76cm routes. These were the 17.5km *Vellachtalbahn* from Kühnsdorf to Eisenkappel and the 29km *Gurktalbahn* between Treibach-Althofen and Klein Glödnitz. Both lines connected with the main line network near Klagenfurt.

Despite its relatively short length, the *Vellachtalbahn* carried quite a considerable amount of timber traffic. Consequently, the first of the Kh Class 0-10-0Ts, no. 499.01, was acquired in 1924 to assist the two T Class 0-6-2Ts that had been the original motive power. Following WW 2, the latter were replaced with P Class 0-8-2Ts nos 199.02 and 199.03 plus some of the Franco-Belge KDL 11 type 0-8-0Ts nos 699.101, 699.103, 699.104 and 0-8-0TT no.699.01. During the 1950s all except the P Class locomotives were fitted with Giesl Ejectors. The Kühnsdorf line closed in 1971, having lost its passenger service in 1965.

The *Gurktalbahn* led an undistinguished life until it succumbed to rationalisation and was closed to passenger traffic in 1968 and freight in 1972. However, a 3.5 km stretch of the line at Treibach- Althofen has been preserved as a "museum line" by the *Verein der Kartner Eisenbahnfreunde* (VKEF) or Carinthian Railway Enthusiasts Society. Since its inception, the VKEF has built up a huge collection of locomotives and rolling stock. In addition to items from the ÖBB network, they have also preserved many industrial locomotives and associated items of rolling stock.

The former ÖBB 76cm gauge locomotives in the collection have included at various times 0-6-2T no.298.102, Uh Class 0-6-2T no.498.02, Yv Class 0-6-4T no.598.01, P Class 0-8-2T no. 199.02, Kh Class 0-10-0T no.499.01 and KDL type 0-8-0T no.699.101. The final three worked on both Carinthian narrow gauge lines during their working lives. Another interesting addition is a 0-6-0T built by Krauss in 1926 for the *Kreis Kreuznachen Kleinbahnen* in Germany and requisitioned by the armed forces for their *Heeresfeldbahn.* Following the end of the war, it was acquired by the ÖBB and numbered 898.01 for use on the *Gurktalbahn*. Some of the locomotives, such as 298.102 and 498.02 have been transferred to other preservation schemes whilst 598.01 now resides on a plinth at Eichgraben in Carinthia.

6.33   The joint standard gauge and 76cm gauge station at Völkermarkt- Kühnsdorf in Carinthia is where 0-8-0T no. 699.104 was seen preparing to depart for Eisenkappel in August 1964. Steam was still in use on the main line at that time, a large tank locomotive can be seen in the background heading towards Klagenfurt. (M. Grandguillaume/BVA)

6.34 *P Class 0-8-2T no.199.02 leaves Kühnsdorf with a freight train bound for Rechberg in August 1964. This locomotive was originally supplied to the Obergrafendorf to Gresten line in 1926, following its extension to Gresten in that year. (M. Grandguillaume/BVA)*

6.35 *No. 199.02 passes Sittersdorf with the same freight train in August 1964. As was so often the case, the freight is carried in standard gauge wagons, mounted on "piggy back" vehicles, which tower above the locomotive. (M. Grandguillaume/BVA)*

6.36   *Franco-Belge KDL 11 Class 0-8-0T no.699.104 has just arrived at Miklauzhof with a mixed train in August 1964. These excellent locomotives, built for the German military railways in 1944, proved to be a valuable asset when transferred to the Austrian narrow gauge lines following the end of hostilities. (M. Grandguillaume/BVA)*

6.37   *One of the KDL 11 Class 0-8-0Ts hauls a passenger train, through the delightful gorge between Miklauzhof and Rechberg, on the same occasion. (M. Grandguillaume/BVA)*

6.38   Nos 699.101 and 199.02, pose in the wooded valley near Rechberg. The Giesel Ejector fitted to the 0-8-0T is clearly shown in this view photographed in August 1964. (M. Grandguillaume/BVA)

6.39   This is the southern terminus of the Kühnsdorf line at Eisenkappel. 0-8-0T no. 699.104 is about to depart with a passenger train, bound for Völkermarkt-Kühnsdorf, in August 1964. (M. Granduillaume/BVA)

Bregenzerwaldbahn

In the extreme west of Austria is the town of Bregenz on the shore of Lake Constance. Until 1983, Bregenz was connected to Bezau by a very scenic 36km narrow gauge line. Running through a deep gorge for much of its route, the *Bregenzerwaldbahn* was a popular line easily accessible from Switzerland and Germany in addition to visitors from Austria. Although diesel traction had replaced steam by 1963, it was thought that steam hauled trains would generate even more interest in the line. With the former locomotives unavailable, the Borsig 0-10-0TT was hired from "Eurovapor", who had purchased this locomotive from the *Zillertalbahn,* in 1974. This was joined in 1978 by KDL11 0-8-0TT no. 699.01 from "Club 760". Sadly, the tourist traffic wasn't sufficient to save the line from closure, which occurred in 1983. In fact it was a landslide in the gorge that finally sealed its fate.

The line lay dormant until 1987 when a preservation group, the *Verein Bregenzerwald-Museumbahn*, was formed to restore the upper 6km of the route near Bezau as a tourist attraction. Two of the line's original locomotives, U Class 298.25 and Uh Class 498.03, were acquired and restored to working order, the latter having stood on a plinth at Bezau for some years. These have since been joined by Uh Class 498.08 and two diesel locomotives nos 2091.04 and 2091.08. Since 1990, a summer weekend service has operated over this short length of line. Although running through a picturesque route, sadly the more dramatic lower section of the line is not available for use. However this now forms part of a footpath and is easily traced.

6.40   The first locomotive to haul tourist trains on the Bregenzerwaldbahn, *in the extreme west of Austria, was Borsig 0-10-0TT no.4. This, former SKGLB, locomotive was hired by the ÖBB from Eurovapor in 1974, who had purchased it from the Zillertalbahn a short time before. The large German locomotive is seen at Jenbach shortly before it was transferred to its new base. After the upper section of the line reopened in 1987, the service was reinstated by the Verein Bregenzerwald-Museumbahn with 0-6-2Ts of both U and Uh Class as motive power. (J.K. Williams)*

6.41   Following a visit to the ÖBB works at Knittelfeld, U Class 0-6-2T no.298.24 was seen on the end of a long standard gauge freight train, whilst being returned to its home depot at Garsten on 11th September 1958. (D. Trevor Rowe)

CONCLUSION

Despite the many closures of the recent past, much of the Austrian narrow gauge network has survived. The independent companies must be applauded for maintaining their services despite mounting competition from road transport and ever increasing operating expenses. Whilst the ÖBB has had to bow to pressure from higher authority and close its unprofitable lines, it is gratifying that some energetic preservationists have saved many sections of line that would have otherwise have been lost without trace. These dynamic organisations have also saved many locomotives and much rolling stock for posterity.

It was perhaps fortunate that when steam was withdrawn from the majority of ÖBB lines during the 1970s, a large number of locomotives were preserved on plinths at appropriate stations throughout the country. Many of these have now been removed from their static retirement and restored to working order. With a result, over 80 Austrian narrow gauge steam locomotives have been preserved, a large proportion of which are in regular service.

Details of the principal independent railways, museum railways and preservation groups that offer a regular steam hauled service can be obtained from the following:-

Achenseebahn.A.G., Bahnhof, A-6200 Jenbach. Tel (0043) 5244 62243.

Club 399, Verein der Freunde der Pinzgaubahn, Brucker Bundesstrasse 21, A-5700, Zell am See.

Club 598, Freunde der Ybbstalbahn, Höhenstrasse 49, A-3340, Waidhofen an der Ybbs.

Club 760, Verein de Freunde der Murtalbahn, Postfach 51, A- 8850, Murau.

Eisenbahnklub Mh6, Werkstättenstrasse 18, A-3200, Obergrafendorf.

Feistritztalbahn Betriebs GmbH, Hauptplatz 13, A-8190, Birkfeld. Tel (0043) 3174 450720.

ÖGEG Steyrtalbahn, Steyrstrasse 11, A-4594 Grünburg. Tel (0043) 664 3812298.

ÖGLB, Österreichische Gesellschaft für Lokalbahn, Poschgasse 6, A-1140, Wien.

Reisebüro der Steiermärkische Landesbahnen, Am Bahnhof, A-8850, Murau. Tel (0043) 3532 2233.

Stainzerbahn, Marktgemeindamt Stainz, A-8510, Stainz. Tel (0043) 3463 220312.

Verein Bregenzerwaldbahn, A-6941, Langenegg 39. Tel (0043) 5513 6192.

Verein de Kärtner Eisenbahnfreunde, Gurktalbahn, Postfach 181, A-9010, Klagenfurt.
Tel (0043) 4262 4783 or (0043) 4229 3528.

Waldviertler Schmalspurbahnen, Bahnhofstrasse 59, A-3871, Alt Nagelberg.
Tel (0043) 6991 146 5350.

Zillertaler Verkehrsbetrieb AG, A-6200 Jenbach. Tel (003) 5244 6060.

Ffestiniog Travel, Harbour Station, Porthmadog, LL49 9NF (Tel:- 01766 516050) provide a comprehensive continental rail ticket service. They can also assist in planning a "tailor made" itinerary to suit any individual requirements. Destinations in Austria are often included in their European holidays, which include some of the lines covered in this publication. However, they cannot issue tickets for the independent and museum railways listed above, which have to be purchased locally.